DESTINATIONS & DISCOVERIES

A Short Collection of Literary Travel Essays

DESTINATIONS & DISCOVERIES

A Short Collection of Literary Travel Essays

EDITED BY
MEGHAN O'NEILL

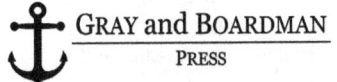
Gray and Boardman
PRESS

Copyright © 2014 by Meghan O'Neill
All rights reserved.
Published in the United States by Gray and Boardman Press
www.grayandboardman.com

Library of Congress Control Number: 2014949854

ISBN: 978-0-9906754-6-4
Printed in the United States of America

Design by Soundview Design Studio
Copyedited by Martha M. Bullen

10 9 8 7 6 5 4 3 2 1

First Edition

Credits

"Will Fish For Love" © 2014 by Elizabeth M. Collins.
Printed by permission of the author.

"Clothing Optional: Shedding the Past at Wreck Beach"
© 2014 by Vicki Valosik. Printed by permission of the author.

"The Irish Detour" © 2014 by Derek Perkins.
Printed by permission of the author.

"The Art of Packing" © 2014 by Bonnie Foote.
Printed by permission of the author.

"How to Survive a Storm" © 2014 Annie Mahon,
Rawmindfulness.com. Reprinted by permission of the author.

"A Walk on the Wicklow Way: A Wanderlust on the Irish
Coast to Coast" © 2014 by Sylvia Bailey Shurbutt.
Printed by permission of the author.

"Lessons from an Italian Mother" © 2014 Marilyn Campbell.
Printed by permission of the author.

"You Say You Want a Revolution" © 2012 by Johanna
Droubay. Previously published in *The Potomac Review*, no 51.
Reprinted by permission of the author.

To all of those who have the courage to put pen to paper (or fingers to keyboard) and bare their souls through writing.

Acknowledgements

We give grateful thanks to the writers, Elizabeth, Vicki, Derek, Bonnie, Annie, Sylvia, Marilyn and Johanna, who shared their stories, travel experiences and reflections in this book. Additionally, we thank Martha Bullen and Paul Mahon.

Contents

Introduction ix

Will Fish For Love 1
By Elizabeth M. Collins

Clothing Optional:
Shedding the Past at Wreck Beach 13
By Vicki Valosik

The Irish Detour... 25
By Derek Perkins

The Art of Packing 29
By Bonnie Foote

How to Survive a Storm 35
By Annie Mahon

A Walk on the Wicklow Way:
A Wanderlust on the Irish Coast to Coast 43
By Sylvia Bailey Shurbutt

Lessons from an Italian Mother 61
By Marilyn Campbell

You Say You Want a Revolution 69
By Johanna Droubay

Contributors' Notes.. 91

INTRODUCTION

I feel humbled to have had the opportunity to read and review the submissions for this book of travel essays. Reflecting on each manuscript has given me extraordinary pleasure and insight. I've taken amazing journeys without leaving the comfort of my cozy reading chair.

This collection of writing is varied in both style and geography. From transforming the first flutters of an idea into the well-crafted words that comprise the essays in this book, each writer has demonstrated not only an obvious adventure, but heart and mind-opening lessons.

The truths and transformative experiences expressed in each essay prove that life-altering travel does not always involve exotic locations. These writers inform, instruct and inspire with stories that they dare to tell others about themselves. I hope our readers will enjoy these vicarious journeys.

Meghan O'Neill

Will Fish For Love

By Elizabeth M. Collins

It's official: I'm a killer. Worse, I'm a baby killer.

I'm wracked with guilt and shame. Even now, long after the crime, I see my victim's tiny pink-orange body whenever I close my eyes, its little fin sticking straight up in the indigo-blue waves.

It was a terrible waste of a perfectly beautiful day in Cabo San Lucas, Mexico. It's not as though I turned to my husband, John, and said, "Do you know what would be fun? Waking up at five in the morning while on vacation and spending the entire morning tossed around in a tiny, smelly Panga fishing boat instead of lying by the pool with margaritas."

It was barely one hour into a five-hour

fishing trip and I had already racked up quite a resume, or maybe a rap sheet: First I committed murder, then I stabbed my hand on the fishing hooks John had stashed in my purse, and next I dozed off, almost falling overboard when we hit a swell larger than our boat. I also had to pee — badly — and the boat didn't have anything resembling a bathroom, so I was looking at a long morning of leg crossing and dehydration.

Fishing is to John what shopping is to me — a way to both relax and waste hundreds of dollars. He is a walking advertisement for the sport, wearing T-shirts decorated with smallmouth bass and blue marlin and, to my horror, a baseball cap ornamented with a real fishing hook, the offending object slipped over the bill, screaming "Redneck. Country Boy. Hick."

He had mentioned the upcoming trip for months, each time Cabo's fish-laden turquoise-to-cobalt water was featured on one of his favorite fishing shows. Because we get two fishing channels and a third outdoor station that's half-fishing, half-hunting at our house, I was sick of everything fishing-related long before our plane had landed.

Nothing would have kept him on shore, however, so it was go along or spend the day alone, staring at the clock, alternately fuming and worrying because John was sure to be hours late. At some point, I would have attempted to use my rusty high school Spanish to telephono Silverados Sport Fishing Charters and the Federales to make sure his boat, the Sushi Time I, hadn't capsized (or been seized by drug smugglers). Then there would have been the inevitable vacation-destroying fight after he casually strolled in as though nothing was wrong, like the time he went fishing for "four hours" and came home the next morning.

That's what happens when a prima donna city girl falls in love with a redneck outdoorsman. I can't claim that I didn't know what I was in for, either, that I didn't know I would have to share John with his scaly mistress, because one of our first dates was a flounder-fishing trip. I refused to touch the slimy bait of eels and guts, or the one weird, brown-speckled fish called a sea robin that I caught and whose life we spared. Anxious to look cute for my new boyfriend, who was happy to bait my hook, I wore a hot pink hoodie and pink, polka dot skimmer shoes with what John called "Grace Kelly" sunglasses. The fishing captain thought I was hilarious.

I'm fairly certain our Mexican captain, Miguel, agreed, but was too nice to laugh at my diamond hoops and inability to recognize a bite. I would much rather have lounged around the boat, sunbathed, and read a trashy romance, but by then I had learned that fishing captains actually get offended if you don't want to come away covered in fish guts. I can't imagine why.

I knew when I was beat though, so I reluctantly grabbed a pole and half-heartedly cast into the sea. Miguel told me I had a "fish on" and John said it could die if I brought it in too slowly. They urged me to reel faster

... faster ... faster ... until the moment a salmon-colored red snapper, glistening in the golden, early morning sun, burst from the water. I cringed to see a second fish on the line — her hungry baby, I assumed, which had followed its mother in search a tasty snack — and I pulled them in with the little strength remaining in my aching, straining muscles. Miguel dismissed the baby as "not a keeper" and tossed it overboard. It flopped once, twice, before floating motionlessly, a beacon on the otherwise midnight Pacific.

As a girl who prefers to believe all food comes in tidy, plastic-wrapped packages, I was particularly horrified when no sooner had John said, "He'll get eaten by someone," than a dark, sharp-eyed sea bird swooped down and disposed of the evidence in its belly. "He's got dinner," John added approvingly.

I'm a terrible, terrible person, I thought, overwhelmed by the Catholic-school guilt that perpetually lives in my stomach — and

Miguel was hardly helpful. He beheaded and skinned several fish alive less than two feet from where I shrank into my once-white vinyl seat, attempting to avoid the blood that splattered all over the deck before eventually landing on John's shoe, eerily reminded of the scene where Anne Boleyn loses her head in "The Tudors."

Grateful that I had skipped breakfast, I prepared to go to confession to exorcise the sight, expecting a penance of a hundred or a thousand "Hail Marys" for the poor creatures' souls and perhaps some community service on behalf of fish rights. And I still had to go to the bathroom. Please let it be over soon, I prayed, recrossing my legs, checking my watch for the hundredth time, and staring, glassy-eyed, at the horizon. Get me off this boat.

My accomplice John had no such qualms, even having two of the snapper cooked at a local restaurant for dinner that night. Practically smacking his lips, he said, "This is the best fish I've ever had," and "Now that's fresh fish," over and over again as he cut through our grilled victims — skin, head, and all — and tried to force-feed me a bite.

"Stop. You know I don't like fish," I replied, recoiling and picking at my steak, offended by the fish — my victims — and by the meal in general. I thought seventeen dollars was just too expensive for a meal when we had provided the main dish, although the chef did remove the snappers' big, bubble-shaped eyes so they couldn't stare at us accusingly. Maybe seventeen dollars was worth it after all — if you don't add in the two-hundred-fifty-dollar fishing trip.

I've been deep-sea fishing with John three or four times, and have sat and read while he fished in countless lakes, ponds, and rivers, but until that day's bloodbath, we had never caught much. "I'm cursed," I joked more than once as we sat and baked on boats, waiting for hours to catch one measly barracuda on our honeymoon in Aruba and the single roosterfish we lured (and released) the first time we were in Cabo. We finally broke the streak on our second Cabo trip, massacring a dozen red snapper and barracuda between us — hours of sheer boredom broken by minutes of excitement, leaving a lifetime of guilt. For me at least, as I reluctantly reeled in the snapper's siblings, cousins, and friends.

"See, you're not bad luck," John said, grinning and looking happier than I've ever seen him as he made plans to go out with Miguel again the next time we're in Cabo. Damn, I thought, dodging the pelicans that swarmed the Sushi Time I in a multi-pronged attempt to snatch the fish bodies. I desperately avoided their beaks and reminded myself why I was out there, that John would do anything for me.

He moved to Maryland from New Jersey when I got a new job, drove me back up to New York City for doctors' appointments, and regularly sacrifices his dignity to carry my purse around the mall. So when the time comes, I'll groan, but then

I'll grab a fishing pole and get the camera ready to photograph the next big catch, the next victim.

Although ... most of my photographs from that last trip focused on the stark contrast between Cabo's postcard beaches and the barren, empty desert beyond — not the crime scene. Miguel pointed out multimillion-dollar mansions owned by the likes of John Travolta that grew out of the cliffs like a luxury, modern-day Pueblo village, and I snapped what looked like a lighthouse-cum-fort — probably an old Spanish castillo once charged with protecting Baja California.

Happy for a distraction from both my conscience and my bladder, I held on as Miguel maneuvered the boat as close to Cabo's famous Arco as he could without capsizing in the roiling water or dashing us on the strange and beautiful rocks. El Arco is a stunning natural arch that rises from the depths where the Sea of Cortez meets the Pacific and marks Land's End.

The rocks surrounding it house thousands of crabs, hundreds of snapper-stealing sea birds on the lookout for a meal, and a colony of lazy, sun-worshiping sea lions that smell of rotten fish. It's also a haven for lucky-charm dolphins that Miguel knew instinctively how to find. (They too follow the fish.) A couple of the friendly, bottlenosed creatures frolicked so close to the boat that we could have reached out and touched them. John and I looked at each other and smiled.

Okay — I admit it. I enjoyed that part. It was even kind of romantic — especially later when I got my margarita. And when John bought me a pretty new necklace.

"Thank you for coming," he said, kissing me gently. "It means a lot."

A month or so later, my mom and I were walking through J.C. Penney when I came across a stack of fishing T-shirts on sale. I ended up buying four different styles for John — including one with a mug shot of a bass, and another that read "Lucky fishing shirt. Do not wash." If only they had come in pink, I might have bought one for myself — maybe.

Clothing Optional: Shedding the Past at Wreck Beach

By Vicki Valosik

As I sit back against one of the many logs washed up at odd angles across Wreck Beach, a rugged stretch of sand thirty minutes from downtown Vancouver, I feel my courage growing. Sandwiched between a steep cliff lined with Douglas firs, the dark waters of the Strait of Georgia, and the white-tipped mountains beyond, Wreck Beach feels surprisingly remote.

Despite the fact that the easiest way to access the beach is via 473 steep wooden steps built into the 200-foot cliff face, a generous sprinkling of people are out enjoying the May sun. A few feet away, a woman swirls a hula hoop up and down her sinewy frame, lost in the silent rhythm of her earbuds. A middle-aged couple lean against a large black rock strumming guitars, while behind them a bearded Ghandi-esque man massages the shoulders of a female laying prone in the sand.

And all of them are naked.

In fact, my husband, Khair, and I are among the few beachgoers wearing anything more than an expression of sun-soaked contentment. I've slipped off my street clothes in favor of my two-piece, while Khair, who was born and raised in the Middle East, sits next to me with his yellow and black swim trunks enveloping him from waist to knee like a security blanket.

In planning a few days of vacation in Vancouver, I discovered "clothing optional" Wreck Beach. On the fringe of University of British Columbia's campus, it was described as an inclusive hangout for sun worshipers, graying hippies, and full-time naturists, and seemed like a welcoming place for the uninitiated — like us.

When I told Khair my idea to share our first public denuding while on vacation, he laughed nervously but didn't say no. The idea gained momentum, and though I hate to admit it, the thing I was soon looking forward to most on an itinerary including kayaking, zip-lining, a visit with West Coast family members, and even a ride in a sea plane, was shedding our clothes in front of dozens of strangers.

As our trip approached, though, what began as hankering for a novel vacation experience grew to take on personal significance. Khair and I have both traveled far from our religious and cultural upbringings, his Syrian Muslim and mine Southern Christian. I was hoping the trip to Wreck Beach would be nothing less than a literal and symbolic shedding of past constraints.

Growing up going to church twice a week and attending a private Christian school, I was never in the habit of wearing anything too short or too tight, and when Khair and I met in college and started dating, I began erring on the side of even looser and longer. Though he never asked for these changes, knowing Khair was raised Muslim, it seemed like the culturally sensitive thing to do. In Khair's background, men, as well as women, dressed conservatively. I knew from the way he avoided bathing for days at a time just to avoid his all-male dorm's communal showers that he still carried the modesty of his Middle Eastern culture with him.

But graduate school — mine in sociology and his in medical science — made us both rethink many of the cultural norms we used to accept and to begin relying on conclusions we reached through logic instead. We questioned our cultures and religions, and, ultimately, we rejected many of the taboos placed on the human body. We came to see it simply as a vessel for living.

On the outside, the changes in our belief system are modest – Khair no longer emerges from swimming pools with a wet t-shirt clinging to his body, and I've retired my tankini in favor of a bikini top – but inside we've become completely different people. Now at a nude beach, where we are severely overdressed in our swim attire, I wonder if we'll have the courage to externalize these changes.

"I think she's selling drinks," Khair says, trying to act normal, and nods toward a young woman wearing nothing but the bandana balancing the neat pile of dreadlocks on top of her head. She smiles as she approaches, her tiny nose ring catching the light. "Hi. What would you like?" the woman asks in a perky voice.

Reaching into her padded cooler for the requested Stella Artois, something in the distance catches her eye; she quickly ducks beside me as a short expletive escapes her lips. "The cops are here!" Then, eyeing our pile of clothes, she asks, "Can you hide my cooler?"

She explains, never taking her eye off the blue-vested police who stand out in ridiculous contrast with the sea of flesh tones, that selling or possessing alcohol on the beach is illegal and comes with a hefty fine. I want to ask this naked stranger about the fine for aiding and abetting, but instead we dutifully pile our jeans and backpacks on top of her cooler.

She introduces herself as Yaana, an undergraduate student at UBC. Then, glancing at the swimsuits still clinging to our bodies and no doubt sensing our newbie jitters, says, "It must be your first time here."

We nod and she gives us the lay of the land, pointing out a group of leathery babyboomers sitting in folding chairs surrounded by giant metal sun reflectors. "They're regulars," she tells us, the ones who enforce proper nude beach etiquette: no photos, no leering, no overt sexual activity.

I have always thought of nude beaches as somewhat deviant — dens of frolicking hedonists practicing their breezy bacchanalia. While Wreck Beach does have a relaxed, lawless vibe, it's more in the vein of skipping out on a parking ticket than of indecent exposure.

Even with the abundance of naked bodies, I am surprised at how the atmosphere feels decidedly nonsexual. In fact, the website admonishes beach visitors — an estimated 500,000 annually — to "Show the public that nude is not lewd" and encourages families to visit. Near us, two women shaded by a sheet propped up with a stick take turns breastfeeding a baby and watching a toddler.

Yaana asks if we will be staying for sunset. "That's when the sun worshippers come out," she says. "They play the drums every night to tell the sun goodbye." After watching the blue dots disappear back up the forested stairs, Yaana bids us farewell and stands to resume her rounds.

We had unknowingly picked a heavily trafficked spot on the way to the "restroom," a trio of fully exposed urinals and a squatty potty with only three walls. A steady parade of birthday suits passes us, fascinating Khair, a medical scientist, with the endless variety of human anatomy. "They really come in all shapes and sizes," he says more than once.

Some wear their nudity majestically, like a shimmering evening gown, and others comfortably, like a favorite pair of sweatpants. One petite blond walks past wearing nothing but knee-high white leather boots. Another woman more stout in posture passes near us, wrapped in a chic Indian sari that completely covers her shoulders and upper body, but stops just above her bare buttocks.

Encouraged by how comfortable everyone seems, I slip off my bikini top. I look at Khair from the corner of my eye, trying to gauge his reaction. After all, it is a big deal for an Arab man, even one as open minded as Khair, to watch his wife take off her top in public. I think back to how he used to gently pull my shirt down if I showed a sliver of back when bending over, and how horrified he was at our American wedding reception when he had to throw the garter belt from my thigh to a group of bachelors. But now, seeing me topless doesn't even cause him to flinch, and we resume our conversation as I spread 70 SPF on my newly exposed skin.

"Are you going to take off your swimsuit?" I ask.

"Maybe later," Khair says, then changes the subject. "Do you want to go see what they're selling?" He nods toward a stall of bohemian clothes flapping in the breeze. I suspect he's really just looking for something to do besides remove his drawers, but I agree. We walk over to where women are trying on ten-dollar dresses in front of a mirror. It strikes me as funny how no dressing room is needed since everyone is already naked. I pick out a long sundress and Khair buys a hemp shirt. As we head back to our spot, I notice a group setting up a drum circle and the way the sun is getting lower in the sky.

I'm suddenly afraid that we might miss our chance. In my mind we're just a thin nylon barrier away from some great epiphany. As soon as we sit down, I grab the skirt of my bathing suit bottom and nod towards Khair's swim trunks.

I look him in the eye and ask, "Well?"

"I am okay with taking them off. I don't have to prove it," he responds somewhat smugly.

"Yes you do!" I exclaim, exasperated. "Saying you are okay with it is not the same as doing it."

I am tired of talking about how open we are. I know from experience that saying we were okay with shedding our clothes in public is a far cry from acting on it. Two years ago when we went to Jamaica for my 30th birthday, Khair and I planned to take the boat out to our resort's nude island, but kept finding excuses. In truth we only thought we were ready.

I pull off my swimsuit bottom, the same skirted bottom I bought years ago for its modest coverage, and wait.

I look at Khair. He looks at the water.

I feel only partially relieved to have finally done it. I want my husband on this journey with me. I realize I want to see that he is okay with who we have become.

Finally Khair says, "Oh, what the hell?" and pulls off his trunks with the crooked half-smile he gets when he does something a little crazy.

The sun's low slant illuminates our bodies in a golden hue, my pale skin glowing against his olive complexion. We lean back against the log, facing the reddening horizon above the water, and Khair takes my hand. There is no great epiphany, just a sense of contentment sitting here together facing the water, nothing between us but the air. Like the good Lord made us, I might have said years ago.

After a few minutes, the horizon is covered with streaks of brilliant red and orange. We hear the drums start, faintly at first and then growing louder. A crowd begins to gather, drawn to the beat a few yards away. Khair and I look at each other. "Let's get out of here before they start chanting," he says, and we both laugh.

We stand to get dressed, shaking the sand off each layer of clothes. We both know that we've removed something more than our swimsuits ... something we won't be putting back on.

What we uncovered, though, was there all along.

The Irish Detour

By Derek Perkins

Ten years ago my wife and I, along with our thirteen-year-old daughter, spent a week biking along the coast of Ireland from Galway to Cork. It rained each day of our trek. The rainfall was gentle and misty, but by the end of each day we were soaked.

Not unexpectedly, my daughter complained endlessly about the dampness. Near the end of our trip, we'd all become accustomed to the weather and it felt familiar and even refreshing. It also made us appreciate a warm bath and a cozy meal. We took those things for granted at home, but after a day-long ride in the rain, they felt like luxuries.

The most scenic part of our journey was the Ring of Kerry, a route that meanders around the Iveragh Peninsula. The lush green landscape and rocky coastline looked like an endless postcard. Filled with stone walls, sheep and cows grazing, it was the part of the country that one envisions when thinking of Ireland.

Early one evening, we rode through a tiny town of Waterville. Water still drizzled from the grey sky. A yellow bed and breakfast stood out in overcast landscape. The sight of it was refreshing, almost uplifting, but we'd planned to spend the night in a small town just a few miles up the road at an inn that promised breathtaking views of the sea below.

We pedaled on, but a few yards up the road, my teenage daughter asked if we could turn around. She felt an unusual attraction to that bright golden building. Surprised and pleased that she had finally found something pleasant on our trip, my wife and I obliged.

We were greeted at the door by the inn's grandfatherly proprietor and his no nonsense wife. They took one look at our soaking wet clothing and dripping hair and invited us in to sit by the fire where they served us hot tea and small bowls of lamb stew.

We inhaled the tea and slurped down the stew, not realizing until that moment how weary we had become. Eating the savory stew felt like wrapping ourselves in a warm blanket. As the smoke from the fire filled our nostrils, the crackling filled our ears and the tea and stew filled our bellies, we felt energized and nourished.

The couple chatted with us about our journey and about our lives in America. They told us they had a thirteen-year-old granddaughter and asked our daughter about school and sports. We helped them wash the dishes and then they sent us to bed with Irish soda bread and more tea.

The next morning there were three places set for us at the dining room table. We ate homemade bread and jam, and the couple packed more soda bread for us to take with us as we continued our journey.

As we prepared to leave, they gave each of us a deeply nourishing hug. We mounted out bikes and rode off into the green landscape, rain drizzling on our heads once more. We didn't want to leave, as this was the Irish experience for which we'd been longing — we just didn't know it.

The Art of Packing

By Bonnie Foote

There is a wizardry to the art of packing, and in it Mary Poppins has nothing on my grandmother.

You begin with a metal frog or similar small toy. This, attached to the outside of your small backpack or purse, is for the entertainment of small children. It clicks when you press it. Eadie's frog has fascinated two- and three-foot-high travelers and natives on every major land mass except Antarctica, where there are no children and the penguins are preoccupied. Of course you have to demonstrate it properly, with both sympathy and sparkle.

It does not take an infinite carpetbag, magic chalk or great physical strength to carry and utilize an aluminum amphibian, though so few people think to do it — she is always surprised about that.

To watch my grandmother, you might think that you need no magic other than childlike wonder, experience and meticulous planning to ensure that you and everyone around you have everything you might need at all times, regardless of the continent, conveyance, or company you find yourself in. If any of your fellow travelers here on this spinning globe are less than delighted with the wonders around you, then you are not doing it properly.

I told Eadie yesterday that I was writing an essay on packing, and she said for the record that I am not qualified. In my defense, I do keep tiny disposable stuffed animals in my everyday backpack, and I have given away several, always with great success (this is mostly facetiously known as the Shut the Small Child Up Initiative), but that is child's play in more than one sense.

You must also master multi-faceted advanced planning for extended stays away from home. One time my brother and I arrived at Eadie's house for Christmas several hours after exams finished.

"I packed sooo badly!" I said. "I just poured my dirty laundry into one plastic bag and my toiletries drawer into another." "Yes, but you used plastic bags," said my brother.

For her trip to Botswana with my parents planned for this October, Eadie had packed her suitcase and carry-on (with two changes of clothing and all necessary toiletries in the carry-on in case of luggage delay) by early June. She would not allow either of these bags to be touched for the road trip to Traverse City later that month. Michigan is not Africa and does not contain its possibilities.

Included in these two bags are three roll-up edifices of toiletries. Like Freud's cities of the mind, they have acquired their contents in slow layers over the years and now include everything. It will be up to my parents, should dinner not go their way exactly, to decide whether or not a Pepto-Bismol tablet expired in 1998 and gone through radiation a few times a year since then will make any digestive problems worse or better in the Botswana spring of late 2014.

Three years ago, when we were on a small-ship cruise off of Guinea Bissau, it took me a bit too long to find the lipstick for cocktail hour. Of course by the time you are on the ship there are not just the three toiletry bags, the nice double-zippered purse, and the everyday small backpack with its eight compartments available for the stashing of small items, but also the nightstand, the closet, any pockets of any pants that have been worn by this point, and the two drawers under the bed.

At that point I suggested that I could help with some editing, perhaps a sweep at categorization and a reduction to two toiletry bags. Apparently. I don't remember the conversation, but I heard this July that my suggestion had been duly considered and rejected, when the Botswana bags were undergoing their third mother-daughter inspection. My mother cheerfully agreed with my grandmother that the system is already wholly logical, and since I won't be along this time, all I have to do is wish Mom luck and attempt to do it sincerely.

At ninety-five, Eadie is, of course, both lucky and brave to be travelling at all, not to mention to be travelling to the wilds of Africa among the elephants and hyenas and mesmerized children, who by this point often think that she is a better attraction than any toy that she carries. The friendliest local little old lady will come up, pat her own white hair, pat my grandmother's white hair, put an arm around her, and suggest a photograph. We are always asked to tell the guide her age, unless the guide knows it already and has repeated it six times since breakfast, which is probable.

Your years are one bit of baggage you cannot leave behind. Until the journey where you need no luggage at all, of course, a journey for which my grandmother is both eager and entirely unprepared. Her parents, brothers, sister, husband, a nephew, a grand-nephew, and most of her friends have embarked already, but so far no postcards. No reservations, no meaningful travel insurance, and since she has seen too much of churches, no known destination.

From any perspective, but especially from this one, even caring about three bags of toiletries and a little metal frog looks very much like courage. Or like magic. Or like art. Elizabeth Bishop knows what we will face at the moment we lose Eadie, but as soon as we can we will focus on the positive, as she has trained us to do.

We have travelled with a hero, wizard, master. That is more than a little something to tuck in your back pocket. It will not take up much room, still, and we might also fit in a Chapstick, perhaps an interesting coin, a crumpled but clean tissue … and a sparkle. And a not-too-terribly-expired Pepto-Bismol.

How to Survive a Storm

By Annie Mahon

Last month, someone asked me how I got a tan on my face in the middle of the winter. So I explained. My 22-year-old daughter Hanna and I were at our mountain cabin during a snowstorm, which dropped two feet of snow there in the Virginia Blue Ridge mountains. It was lovely and idyllic, especially as we sat by the wood stove reading and chatting.

The day after the snowstorm the sun came out, especially so on our upstairs south-facing deck. I wanted Hanna to see how warm that deck could be, even with mounds of snow and 30 degree weather. I went upstairs in my slippers and out onto the deck without putting on a coat. The sun was warm there although it was still below freezing. I called to my daughter, and she came out barefoot and pulled the door closed behind her.

I heard the door closing, but before I could get any words out, it clicked and locked. We were trapped on the second floor deck acres from any neighbors on a mountain in the snow. We had just two slippers between us and no coats. Thank goodness I was right – the deck was warm and sunny even in the cold.

I'll be honest. My first response was toward blaming and shaming. "Why would you close the door all the way when going onto a deck?!" I asked in a louder-than-usual voice.

"Well, you and Dad have always insisted that we not let cold air into the house!" was her rebuttal.

Clearly, blaming wasn't going to get us inside the warm house (where the dogs were relaxing by the fire). We had no phones, no shoes, and no warm clothes. Hanna was in a t-shirt. We faced the mountain with the road down the mountain on the other side of the cabin, and no cars passed by anyway because of the snow. There was one thin edge of deck that wasn't covered in snow. Rather than venting, we dumped the snow out of the two metal chairs and sat down to consider our situation.

For the next hour or so, we tried several techniques. First, I tried to climb down by hanging from the deck and reaching one leg for the flower boxes. After hitting ice under my slippers and almost falling, we decided that was a bad idea. We tried kicking the door individually and together, and even tried to use the chair legs to pry it open. We used both of our slightly different hair clips to try to pick the lock. No luck. Over and over we considered jumping down, but neither of us were brave enough to risk breaking a back or a leg. Even as we discussed it, the snow on the ground was melting, making jumping less safe.

We alternated between laughing about

our predicament and getting serious about the fact that we would freeze if we didn't get inside before nightfall. At one point I suggested that our situation was like the fairy tale Rapunzel, and we laughed about the fact that we wouldn't have enough hair between us to climb down, even if a prince appeared.

Meanwhile, the Dalai Lama's words kept coming back to me:

> *"If a problem is fixable, if a situation is such that you can do something about it, then there is no need to worry. If it's not fixable, then there is no help in worrying. There is no benefit in worrying whatsoever."* — H.H. Dalai Lama.

Remembering this and practicing it kept us in a state of mind to be ready and open to any and all possible solutions. After more than an hour we heard a snow plow up on the mountain and we realized that there must be someone there plowing. So as soon as we heard the engine go off we started to call out. "Hello!" "Can you help us?!" etc.

Eventually we got a response and our nearest neighbor, though he didn't know what we were saying, braved the two feet of snow to hike up to our house. He was able to get into the house, come upstairs and free us from our second floor perch.

Of course it all turned out just fine, and I even got some sun on my face to show for it, but it could have been a lot worse. Yes, we could have frozen out there in the snow, but even if we hadn't frozen, we could have chosen to make ourselves miserable the entire time. We could have shamed and blamed each other and ourselves, or gotten ourselves tied in mental knots. We didn't deny the seriousness of the situation, but I also think we managed not to add any additional suffering to what was already happening.

Buddhists have a story about the second arrow of suffering. We regularly get shot with the arrows of difficulties in our life.

Instead of pulling the arrow out, we shoot ourselves with a second arrow. The second arrow could be our anger about the situation, blaming ourselves or others, worrying or doubting, or even using addictions to distract ourselves. On the deck we mostly experienced the arrow as it was, without adding to it.

Roshi Bernie Glassman offers us three Peacemaker tenants. The first, Not Knowing, and the second, Bearing Witness, invariably lead to the third, Loving Action. Sure, it can be hard to admit we don't know how, give up the drama of blaming and freaking out and sit in the middle of our difficulty. But maybe it's worth it, even in this kind of relatively minor irritation.

After the rescue, Hanna and I were able to seamlessly go back to enjoying the snow and the fire without a lot of drama residue. We joked about it later, but it didn't carry into our lives the way it might have if we had blamed each other or gotten ourselves worked up. We weren't left with any anger between us, and we didn't create any resentment or friction in our relationship.

Having shot myself and others with the drama of the second arrow many, many times, I am slowly seeing how much easier life can be if I simply experience the difficult situation as it is.

A Walk on the Wicklow Way: A Wanderlust on the Irish Coast to Coast

By Sylvia Bailey Shurbutt

My husband Ray and I have a thing about walking rather than driving, traveling by train or biking across a country. A walk slows one down, brings the scenery and the people into focus like no other mode of travel, and an intimate connection is made with the landscape.

Best of all, walking becomes the only raison d'être — all the cares of life fade away and "getting there," just the journey, is significant. If you are walking with a partner, then a bond is formed that is special.

Ray and I have walked the Wainwright English Coast to Coast from St. Bees to

Robin Hood's Bay, the West Highland Way from Glasgow to Fort William, and Hadrian's Wall from Newcastle to Bowness-on-Solway.

I have wanted for years to walk across Ireland, planned, prodded and dropped many hints. Ray finally told me, "I just don't want to walk in the rain!" So . . . I began the journey by myself, the first stage of which is called the Wicklow Way, 80 miles from Dublin to Clonegal.

Here is that journey, day by day, my first long-distance high feld walk alone.

1 August, Dublin to Enniskerry

Walking from Dublin town center to Powerscourt, the first leg of the Wicklow Way on the Irish Coast to Coast, just did not appeal to me. I had already trekked across the city for two days doing some of the touristy things I had not yet done with students on two previous trips to Ireland as part of our Celtic Roots Travel Program at Shepherd University.

So, on 1 August, I hopped a bus for 3 euros and started my journey to Clonegal from Enniskerry, experiencing at the local inn the first of the unexpected culinary surprises that I had not encountered in Ireland before. Starting at Enniskerry, just a mile or so from Powercourt, gave me a day in the famed gardens. And the three days of sunshine so far put my mind at ease about walking in the high mountains across Ireland.

2 August, Powerscourt to Lough Dan

I am blessed—the goddess watches over me! I set off this morning from Knockree to walk about 14 miles to Old Bridge, where I was hoping to find Lough Dan Guest House, a warm and exquisite place where I sit at this moment in time. After three days of mostly sunny Ireland, the mist was not unpleasant as I set off this morning, a taxi carrying me the 7 kilometers from Enniskerry to Knockree, where the Wicklow Way starts in earnest.

The rain was light, and the coolness made for pleasant walking. Happily, the trail was nicely marked, and the maps and directions are excellent in Paddy Dillon's essential book, *The Irish Coast to Coast Walk*. What was best was that, with each turn and twist of the map and my walk, the directions were spot on. I was feeling heady — it was clear that I could do this quite well without Ray, my sturdy walking companion

Then a little after noon, when there was some dispute between my book and the Way posts, I met a biker as I was halfway up my first challenging climb, Djouce Mountain. The biker told me I was surely on the wrong route, and indeed I wasn't anxious to climb the shell-shaped dome looming forbiddingly in the mist. So I headed back down the mountain, loath to retrace my steps but thinking the biker, so sure of himself, must be right.

Thirty minutes later, almost to the stile that had earlier sent me upward, I met two elderly gentlemen from Dublin, who said indeed I had been right to climb upward, but the track would veer after a time along the ridge of the mountain. They said I could join them, which I gratefully accepted. Upward again I trekked, as the rain began to fall in earnest. The route took us over serious bogs that only were walkable by going over "sleepers," as my two old Dubliners told me, which looked like train trestles bolted together to construct a walkway about 18 inches wide to traverse over the bogs.

As we slogged onward, the rain came down in torrents. I must say these old Dubliners were in fine shape, as I had to jog to keep up with them, not at all easy or prudent on the sleepers. I was reluctant to let them out of my sight in the fog, since they had walked the Way before and thus knew the way!

When we came around the last high feld, still walking on the sleepers, an incredible sight appeared: a high lake in the middle of the mountain surrounded by steep cliffs — breathtakingly beautiful. That was Lough

Dan (and this very house I sit in was a tiny speck in the mist far across the valley). I was so drenched by this point and my boots so wet they were foaming and squooshing with each sad step, a sickly sound for a walker. The wind had blasted my umbrella to pieces, my water-resistant jacket had given up trying to keep me dry, but the two old Dubliners tramped on, and I with them.

It was after 4:00 p.m. when we at long last we came to a road, no sign of the rain diminishing, and I was thinking my adventure was becoming tedious if not downright uncomfortable. Then up drove Malachy and Mary—two lovely Irish folk (he a lawyer and she a banker), out traversing the barren heath as there was nothing better to do on such a wet, soggy Saturday, according to Malachy.

Malachy told us that two bikers up the road (whom we had passed earlier) said we might need "rescuing," and they would be happy to drive us to the nearest town of Roundwood. My two Dubliners declined.

Since I didn't have the slightest idea how to get to Lough Dan House where I was to spend the night, and a town sounded most appealing after four hours on the high bogs facing 40 mile-an-hour wind and rain, I hopped in the car.

As it turned out, Sean and Teresa, who own Lough Dan House, were friends with Malachy and Mary, so Malachy was happy to drive me to their doorstep (which by the road was about a 45-minute drive around winding mountain lanes). I am told this is the highest B&B on the Wicklow Way; it is certainly the driest and warmest.

3 August, Old Bridge to Glendalough

Today was the perfect Irish summer day — in other words, overcast and lightly raining, with "sprinkles" of intermittent sunshine. I am now in Glendalough, having walked over a lovely mountain range and descended into this austere valley. Glendalough is the oldest monastic site in Ireland, going back to the anchorite Kevin, who sought a wilderness setting to commune with God. Legend has it that on a day he was praying most earnestly, lost in holy thought, a bird began to build a nest in his outstretched hands. A truly gentle soul, he refused to move until the nest was finished, the eggs laid and hatchlings flown away.

Kevin sought utter isolation, choosing to live in a cave nearby, but it wasn't long before his presence caught the attention of a plethora of faithful followers. Before Andrew could say Amen, the area had blossomed into a religious center, with pilgrims galore. In the 7th Century, the stone ruin that folks see today, with its distinctive round tower, was one of Europe's great cathedrals, such as they were in the 7th Century.

By 1214, Glendalough had ceased to be a great Church center and before long it was just a holy afterthought. I suspect it was because the Wicklow Mountains were just too hard to travel out and about and there were no sleepers to allow an earnest pilgrim a high step through the bogs (the tops of these mountains are filled with great black pools and quicksand, which are treacherous for walkers.)

4 August, Glendalough to Glenmalure

So when the sun shines all day and the sky is cobalt blue, what do the Irish do? They head for a country inn like this one, Glenmalure Lodge, have a lovely meal, and sit out in the sun as they dine. Since I had been in the sun all day, with feet and knees trembling from their trekking across Mullacor and Lugduff Mountains, I sat inside, with my Guinness in hand and roast turkey on the table, recovering from the day's walk — and watching a lovely four-year-old Irish boy who thought he was a rabbit.

The scenery today ranged from inspiring to spectacular. As I left Glendalough early this morning, Kevin's holy ruins were a bit more holy and less crowded, no kids running amongst the gravestones — just a quiet, glistening morning, with sunlight filtering through the trees as I headed up the Green Road and the side of the valley. As I walked, passing Poulanass Waterfall, the scenery got progressively more incredible, until finally I reached the top of Slieve Maan. Those ingenious Irish sleepers helped me cross the high bogs and descend a frighteningly steep side of the mountain and over to Glenmalure Valley.

Glenmalure is the longest glacial valley in Ireland, and simply spectacular: at one point I came to a nameless waterfall that tumbled down the full face of the mountain, reminding me of the high falls in New Zealand that my daughter Rae took her father and me to see in Fiordland National Park. These steep descents do the knees little good. Walking the Wicklow Way is not easy. I wondered what happened to the two Dubliners—it was late when we parted and I accepted the ride from Malachy and Mary to Lough Dan. The Dubliners were walking all the way to Glendalough (which took me another day), so they must have kept walking long after dark.

5 August, Kyle Farm at Moyne

Wherever I go, people ask, as they did just now at Kyle Farm where I rest on the Wicklow Way: "Are you traveling alone? Why?" Seamus Heaney's poem "St. Kevin and the Blackbird" captures some of why this experience is so appealing. Heaney tells us of St. Kevin who is completely unaware of self as the bird proceeds to build its nest in his supplicant hands. In the poem, Kevin is utterly removed from anything superfluous, from the day-to-day trivia that fills and consumes our lives. He is nothing in his time of prayer, and he is everything.

When one walks, there is only one step in front of the other and one's rhythmic breathing. When one walks, there are no worries, no concerns beyond the view, an occasional pain or the map — life is immensely simple. There are no deadlines, no papers to be graded, no best laid plans "gang aft agley" — there is only the walking and the breathing: if my body could do it, I would walk around the world.

But best of all, every sight, sound, and experience is emblazoned in the memory — time is slowed as our pace is slowed; one can go back through the walk and remember every single detail, details impossible in the hurly-burly of living life. When one walks, there is only the moment, and that is enough.

So here I am at the Kyle Farm, about a 17-mile walk from Glenmalure. Much of the Wicklow was by road today. The view from Shielstown Ridge was spectacular, as was the high ridge I climbed leaving Glenmalure this morning, but no better than the view from Kyle Farm patio where I sit enjoying a Heineken while Margaret prepares our evening meal.

This is a working farm, which has been in Margaret's husband's family for seven generations. I suspect the B&B, begun 15 years ago, will help keep the farm going for another generation. There is a family here from Holland, walking from inn to inn as a way to see Ireland, and two other couples exploring the sights in cars. And I walking alone, but not without great pleasure.

6 August, Stoops House at Shillelagh

Yesterday was perhaps my finest walk on the Way, from Kyle Farm to Tinahely. The sky was blue as I set off early morning, down the hill from the dairy farm where I stayed the night with Margaret and her family. It has rained each night, so the Way is wet, but nice to walk in the bright sunshine of day.

On this day I caught up with the Wicklow Way on what the guidebook called "an undulating track." Now, how can you go wrong on such a road? The day was completely delightful, with the track traversing alongside a high ridge with a constantly lovely view. Up and down rolling hillsides, on grassy tracks high above the valley, an inspiring view always present. Bach played on automatic in my brain, and birds and summer sounds accompanied my interior soundtrack.

On a day such as this, all one's senses are heightened, particularly sound. A stream always announces itself, a waterfall is stereophonic. A tractor surprised me as I began the descent toward Tinahely, its sound jarring, as did an Irish deer, small, fearless and seemingly unafraid of me. The two of us communed for a few minutes and I walked on.

Then the village of Tinahely came into view. It looked like only a quarter mile to go (downward, thankfully); in truth, four more miles of a grassy track and backtracking on a road lay ahead. When I finally came to a bridge across a roiling river, it was clear why I still had to walk in the direction I had traveled to reach the town, a fine meal, and the short drive to Stoops Lodge in Shillelagh. I wasn't aware at the time, but this was the end of the Wicklow Way, at least for me.

And then I encountered Bill Mullhall, a wiry, one-legged Irishman who had built Stoops Lodge from a vision in his mind — no plans, just the thinking of it, no formal architectural training (though he is doubtless a master engineer and artist) . . . but a beautiful result. Stoops Lodge is a lovely Victorian-style stone building, with gorgeous pine beams throughout the house, flawless design and appointments and a cascading rock garden that fills the hillside. Bill said he used a common trowel to make his garden.

8 August, Moss Cottage Clonegal

This morning, I asked Denise, Bill's wife, to show me the way to the Forest House for the last little bit of the Wicklow Way, but she didn't know how to reach it by road. So she just took me to Clonegal, the end of the Way. Sometimes the grandest adventures can fade quite away with hardly a notice—or as Eliot says, "end not with a bang but a whimper!"

I had six glorious days walking the Wicklow Way, from Powerscourt to Tinahely. Every day, except the first, has been glorious, sunny weather. The stormy beginning was useful to keep me respectful (fearful) of the power of this place, where the wind can literally sweep you off the mountain. The high bog, virtually impassable without someone's painstaking placement of thousands of sleepers, is formidable and awesome. I can see why the early Gaels used the bogs for their religious doings . . . and why we have found so many treasures and human remains buried in those cold, dark waters.

The work that Ireland has put into the Wicklow Way is simply amazing — and deeply appreciated. Each time I was about to doubt myself, there appeared that tiny yellow arrow with the hiker symbol reminding me I was still on the Way. Walking the Wicklow Way makes one mindful of watching and choosing carefully for the right way.

Editor's Note: More information on the walks mentioned in this essay can be found via these links:

Wainwright English Coast to Coast
http://www.walkingenglishman.com/coast2coast.htm

The West Highland Way
http://www.walkingenglishman.com/westhighlandway01.html

Hadrian's Wall
http://www.nationaltrail.co.uk/hadrians-wall-path

The Wicklow Way
http://www.wicklowway.com/trail-maps/

Lessons from an Italian Mother

By Marilyn Campbell

Carla Ulivieri, a round, gray-haired woman with wire-rimmed glasses, stood in the center of her cluttered 1950s-era kitchen wielding a knife in her right hand. She was pointing it in my direction. With her left hand she scooped up a cluster of sun-ripened heirloom tomatoes from the wood block table and plucked them off the vine one by one. In another fluid motion, she sliced off the green leafy tops. Then, taking each red-orange orb between her large, crooked fingers, she squeezed out the pulp until only a limp form of the fruit remained.

Carla had welcomed me into her home in Florence one Monday afternoon for a private lesson in traditional Tuscan cooking.

Forgoing the corporate culinary schools brimming with wide-eyed American tourists, I had opted for a chance to learn authentic Italian food preparation from an authentic Italian.

If the family is the backbone of Italian society, and the women of the family are the keepers of culinary tradition, then the true epicurean experience can be had only under the guidance of an Italian mother. You just need to find one.

A friend who was studying in Florence at the time introduced me to Carla. Our relationship evolved gradually during my visit with my friend, a self-described foodie. It didn't take long before I considered Carla my own mamma Italiana. One of the reasons that Carla offered culinary guidance so freely was her worry that traditional Italian food preparation was being replaced by modern efficiency. This was a concern, she said, among an older generation of Italian women.

"It takes time to make ragù alla Bolognese," proclaimed Carla. "It has to simmer for five to six hours. If you want to make bread, you have to start baking it the morning if you want it to be ready for lunch. People don't have the time any more."

Carla's fear was that Italian food traditions were becoming a lost art. It was important to her that regional cuisine maintains its own identity. If you want pappardelle pasta with black cabbage pesto, go to Greve, but if fried crostini with chicken and rabbit livers is what you crave, head to Lucca.

I came to understand and appreciate her passion for culinary preservation. And so that sweltering, sunny afternoon, I made my way through Florence on foot to Carla's apartment building on the brownstone-lined Via Leonardo da Vinci, just past the dusty Piazza Savonarola.

I arrived a few minutes early for my two o'clock session. Carla, a woman in her sixties, was just returning from the market with her shaggy mixed-breed dog, Lila. Wearing a breezy housedress with her hair in a loose bun, she bounded up the stairs to her second story flat with her pooch and several bags of groceries in tow. She led me through her home where family photos and reproductions of masterpieces like Vermeer's "Girl with a Pearl Earring" lined the walls.

Once inside her kitchen, my lesson began with tomatoes. Carla's steady and skilled hands demolished the fruit effortlessly. Squeezing out the pulp, said Carla, got rid of extra acidity while preserving the taste. Making her way over to the other side of the kitchen, she plucked a few basil leaves from the potted herb plant in the window sill. She shredded the fragrantly woodsy leaves and tossed them into the bowl. I followed her lead, plucking, shredding, and tossing into my own bowl.

"Cooking has to be fun and it should be an adventure," said Carla as she added fresh vermicelli noodles to the stainless steel cauldron of salted water boiling furiously on her white gas cooktop.

"I do shopping at San Lorenzo's market," she told me, referring to the famous epicurean center a few blocks away. "I buy bread at the bakery and vegetables at a produce stand. All of it is produced locally." Carla could name the origin of each ingredient that comprised our lunch, including the olive oil that was produced by her cousin who owns a farm in Tuscany.

I was fascinated by Carla's grocery shopping habits. A different market for each item was a luxury of time I could not afford. A supermarket sweepstakes-style dash through my local grocery store was about all that my schedule allowed. But Carla said her time-consuming method is vital to the deeply flavored and complex taste of her meals.

Carla didn't take any measurements and only stirred the boiling pot once. A few dashes of salt and a generous slathering of olive oil later, the vermicelli was al dente, and we were finished cooking.

"This is simple," she said referring to

the unnamed salted-tomatoes-and-basil-over-pasta dish that we were preparing. "But if you use great ingredients, the taste is rich."

I wanted to know the key to understanding Italian cuisine. "Each region and village in Italy has its own food style," said Carla, acknowledging the reality that the country is divided into many regions, each as steadfastly united as the Italian family unit. "But bread, wine and olive oil are the backbones of all Italian food."

After my lesson, Carla handed me a blue-rimmed earthenware bowl and led me into her dining room to eat the lunch that we'd just made. The powerful aroma, woodsy basil and nutty olive oil with a hint of pepper, trailed behind us. I plopped down in one of the chairs around her antique lace-covered dining table and tried a fork-full of our creation. The juices from the tomatoes flooded my mouth while the olive oil added a velvety coating that gave the dish an almost creamy texture.

"Where did you learn to cook?" I asked between bites. "I learned from my mother, Norina," she said. "I started cooking after I got married." Carla has been married for 40 years.

She proudly showed pictures of her husband and two children, and underscored the notion that the roots of real Italian food are in the family. And the key to preserving those roots lies not in culinary schools or cookbooks, but in passing down culinary tradition from mother to daughter.

You Say You Want a Revolution

By Johanna Droubay

For months I was just a girl he called for sex. Whenever he called, wherever I was, I would go to him. I left class in Paris's Sixth Arrondissement to meet him at his friend's apartment in the Seventh. We made love in the bathroom while his friend played video games a wall away. In the Ninth, I hurried through my host mother's elaborate dinners — confit du canard, moules marinières, fondu bourguignonne — to meet him at his parents' place in the Nineteenth. We fooled around in the concrete stairwell while his mother folded his clothes in the living room. Six, seven, nine, nineteen. As Paris's twenty arrondissements spiral out from the city center, I spiraled away from a center, too. It was no use trying to control the situation.

When I dared to be the caller instead of the called, he almost always made up some excuse: he was in Florence marching against capitalism; he was in the banlieue flyering for peace. I didn't mind exactly. I liked longing for him. I liked the urgent feeling of our encounters, encounters that I could neither plan nor predict. Encounters that left me exhausted and full of sweet despair.

I was twenty, a junior from Reed College in Oregon, and despite my fluency in the universal language, my French was very bad. In fact, my sophomore-year French professor's tepid recommendation had nearly barred my acceptance into my year-long study abroad program. I suppose he was right to doubt my academic seriousness. But I was serious about other things: writing in my journal, assembling outfits, learning to roll cigarettes and pick up men. And because I was on the verge of adulthood, I believed I was also on the verge of becoming serious about something else. Something important, even revolutionary.

I first met Adrien at 3 a.m. under the Simone-de-Beauvoir footbridge on the left bank of the Seine, many miles south of my host mother's apartment near Montmartre. It was early October 2002, and Paris was hosting its first Nuit Blanche, a citywide celebration lasting from sunset to sunrise. My American friends had all gone back to their dorms at the Cité Universitaire, but I had stayed behind to shiver in the company of drum circlers and fire dancers, convinced that I belonged among them.

"Vous avez du feu?" I asked, thumbing an invisible lighter. The slender twenty-something I addressed had buzzed hair and thick eyebrows. He was handsome and pale, white like stone, with a sharp nose, dark eyes, and high cheekbones. My request interrupted a heated conversation he was having with some friends, with whom he was sitting on the ground, hands stuffed deep in the pockets of his black, hooded sweater.

"T'es contre la guerre?" he asked back, refusing to give me a light until I agreed to oppose my country's second Iraq war, the beginning of which was still five months away.

I nodded.

"Okay," he said.

I crouched down to meet his gaze, and he swiped my cigarette, which he licked and split open lengthwise, emptying its contents onto a rolling paper. He put the flame of his lighter to a little brown hash stone, rubbed it between his fingers, and sprinkled it over the tobacco. Finally he wrapped up the joint and lit it. He took a long, hungry drag, then suddenly withdrew it from his lips.

"Désolé," he apologized and then exhaled. He smiled and looked down, shoving the joint in my direction. "It's yours."

Despite Adrien's self-identification as a militant communist, he didn't always remember to share. His father, a journalist, once chuckled as he told me how Adrien had behaved as a toddler when their family moved for a few years to Soviet Czechoslovakia. It wasn't long before Adrien's parents heard him shouting at his new Czech playmates his first and favorite foreign word: "Moje!" — Czech for "mine."

And yet on mornings when I woke up next to him in his parents' sunny apartment in the Nineteenth, Adrien devoured the collectivist philosophies of Trotsky, Marx, and Engels. As we dressed, as we ate brioche-and-Nutella breakfasts, as we smoked our first cigarette of the day and walked to the Belleville Métro, Adrien plowed through paperback communist classics, hardly looking up except to say, "Pardon."

But I was the one who was spellbound, transfixed by his intensity and hopeful that some of it would rub off. I had spent high school dusting off my dad's collection of Vietnam-War-era records, growing my hair long, and raking through racks at Goodwill in search of the perfect pair of corduroy bellbottoms. Basically communing with the antimaterialist movement of the '60s and '70s by way of the movement's material relics. Now here was this passionate young Frenchman telling me: the revolution is now.

* * *

Adrien's commitment to the revolution, and to his busy schedule of meetings and manifestations, weakened in the presence of only two things: sex and violent video games. Because he had easy access to both, he was late for everything, and so was I. A written evaluation from one of my Parisian professors bears witness: "Johanna is lively and intelligent. What has happened to her this semester? (Absences, missing assignments.) I get the impression that some sort of hardship prevented her from working to her fullest potential."

It wasn't so much hardship as it was weekdays spent in Adrien's bed smoking hash and nuzzling his two calico kittens, whose wrestling we sometimes mimicked. Lazy mornings turned into hazy afternoons as French or American rap music droned in the background. I justified skipping class by turning our rap-listening into a translation exercise, though interpreting Wu-Tang felt like trying to conjugate kisses. Adrien also gleaned lessons from rap, but they were lessons of philosophy, not language.

"Ecoute," he once said, ordering me to listen as he stumbled across the room to pause the CD and replay a line we had just heard.

"Translate," I said from the bed where I lay spread out like jam.

After a moment he said in English, "Okay: Life is a lotto, one chance you will win and a million you will lose."

"Oh," I said, cupping one of the kittens close to my chest. "Life's not like that."

"Si, si," he said. "La vie est la merde. Complete shit."

"No."

"Mais si. Pour la plus part du monde." For most of the world.

Maybe because I was high, maybe because I still treasured my own set of ideals,

I turned my head away from him and cried, quietly so he wouldn't notice. It wasn't that he had changed my mind, though I wanted him to. I wanted to care, the way he did, about the millions of people who suffered through poverty or sickness or discrimination. But I cried only for him, the one I lay next to.

* * *

In April 2003, not long before the general strike that would shut down the city, something caused Adrien to change his mind about me.

In my room on Rue des Martyrs in the Ninth, on a night when my host mother was away with a boyfriend of her own, he asked me, "How many others have you slept with?"

"How many?"

"Since you arrived," he said. "En France."

Only three, I said as innocently as I could. "Seulement trois."

His reaction surprised me. He cuddled me in his arms like one of his kittens and cooed in my ear, "T'es si pur!" So pure? I supposed that, compared with his own number, three was practically adorable.

The next day he surprised me again when he told me he loved me.

"Je t'aime, je t'aime, je t'aime, je t'aime," he said again and again, in bed, on the phone, in the Métro station. I wondered what he could mean. Even without knowing for sure, I couldn't help but say it back.

"Je t'aime," I said. Like everything in Paris, it seemed worth trying.

Later, I don't remember when exactly, I realized he might have misheard me when I numbered my conquests. In sound, the following phrases are indistinguishable:

Seulement trois: only three

Seulement toi: only you

It's possible, in fact probable, that Adrien fell in love with me only when he believed he owned me — quite the opposite of how I felt. I loved him because he had been, until then, uncapturable. I loved him because his untempered self-certainty made me believe he owned himself.

* * *

In June, a month before I would return to the States, Adrien and I made plans to protest the 2003 Group of Eight summit, the annual meeting of first-world leaders to be held that year on the southern shore of Lake Geneva in Evian. Adrien's parents drove us to Gare Montparnasse where we would board a charter bus to a makeshift protesters camp four days before the start of the summit.

His mother, an art teacher, tried once more to persuade him to bring a sleeping bag, but her insistence made him doubly determined to go without. Adrien seemed perpetually annoyed by his mother. Because he was a young man, he felt that she infringed on his independence. And because of his world view, I think he sometimes condemned her for caring more about him than about anyone else.

After an all-night bus trip, we arrived in Annemasse, 10 miles outside of Evian. It was overcast and early when our bus pulled into a field that was spring-green and speckled with lavender, at least where it wasn't overlaid with tents. There were thousands of them, nylon and canvas shelters in every color, but all of a similar size and shape: low-to-the-ground domes that gave the camp, like Paris, a uniform roof line.

We stepped off of the bus and into the soft, gray soil, and I drew in a long breath of mud-and-metallic, leafy country air. I loved Paris, but I had missed nature. I had begun to feel weighed down by Paris's hard stone and concrete, every inch of which man had created, exactly to taste. I preferred a wilder landscape, an old-growth Oregon forest or a mountain valley, like the one that holds Huntsville, Utah, where I grew up. I longed for cliffs that would dwarf me and winds that would quiet me: things that laughed at my aspirations to change my own nature, let alone the world.

While I craned my neck to see from one end of the sky to the other, Adrien bounded toward the center of the camp to stake out his territory and, he declared, to raise a flag. His comrades, fellow members of his activist group Les Resistances, followed after him as he called out specifications: six meters tall and red for revolution.

Before leaving Paris, I had gone on a grocery shopping spree. I knew Adrien wouldn't bring food, and I imagined myself coming to his rescue with all kinds of spectacular treats. I spent 50 euros (half of what I had to live on until my departure at the end of June) on chocolate cereal, Nutella, and brioche; a pound of dark cherries, a can of mangoes, and a jar of raspberry jam; summer sausage, herb cheese spread, and a fresh baguette; special soups and cocktail crackers; boxes of granola bars and bags of candy. I had even found a special American delicacy in an exotic foods boutique: a 10-euro jar of peanut butter. I couldn't wait to unveil these treats one by one on our romantic getaway.

But as soon as we set up our tents, Adrien and his friends decided that we would pool all of our supplies in Benoit's tent, and that Benoit would ration the food, doling out snacks and planning meals as he saw fit.

Typically, I was more than eager to please, more than willing to make sacrifices if it meant fitting in with Adrien's friends and experiencing the real France, the France (I remained smugly convinced) that my American classmates would never know. But as I observed the comrades tossing their half-loaves of sliced white bread and cans of Spaghetti O's onto the pile next to Benoit's sleeping bag, I couldn't help but feel wronged. My head started to ache as Benoit and the others picked through my groceries, laughing at some (the mangoes) and tasting others (the peanut butter).

"C'est trop bon!" Benoit raved as he stuck his finger in the peanut butter for another taste. "Merci, Johanna."

"Je t'en prie," I chirped, retreating to our tent. Instead of resigning myself to share, I vowed to eat none of it. I had a few euros, and that night, while the guys waited for their Chef Boyardee to bubble in the tin they had cut open and placed directly in the camp fire, I disappeared to buy a spicy chorizo sandwich from the camp kitchen, the kitchen our crew had collectively spurned because it recognized government currency as a form of trade.

The next day, after a restless night of sharing my sleeping bag and narrow foam pad with Adrien, I disappeared again to explore the woods that defined the outer limits of the camp. Among the ferns and trees and bowing bluebells the air was thick, almost fizzy, and it popped against my skin like Coke bubbles. Not far from the women's shower, a spot in the woods sectioned off with tarps and equipped with hoses, I sat on a stump and read *Sweet Thursday*, Steinbeck's follow-up to *Cannery Row:*

> It is better to sit in appreciative contemplation of a world in which beauty is eternally supported on a foundation of ugliness: cut out the support, and beauty will sink from sight.

I felt wicked copying this sentence into my journal at the same moment my fellow campers were probably painting signs with pleas on behalf of the world's poor. What would Adrien say? Maybe he would agree with Steinbeck, except for the sitting and appreciating part.

The poor are the world's foundation, he might say, without which the rich are helpless.

But I read it differently. And it made me wonder if Adrien's world, that landscape of stone and concrete ideals, was the kind of world from which ugliness, and along with it beauty, had been excised.

When I emerged from the woods, I found Adrien digging a trench to divert runoff from somewhere, a project that had taken on the import of constructing the Roman aqueducts.

"Tiens," I said when I saw him. "I want you to read something Steinbeck wrote."

"I'm not curious about your books," Adrien barked, and went right on working.

I couldn't help but laugh at the way he said it. Especially after I had spent months clumsily but patiently digesting his library, from Chomsky to Zinn.

"I thought you approved of Steinbeck," I said, nudging him playfully.

Then Adrien grabbed my forearm and pulled me aside. "Where have you been?" he said.

"Reading," I said. I pointed to the trees behind me, "Juste là."

"Not with one of the men you've been flirting with?"

"Quoi?"

"Do you sleep with my friends?" he hissed.

"No," I said firmly, trying to dislodge his grip.

Squeals from the dig site interrupted

our quarrel. The diggers had unearthed a couple of mice, one big and one small.

I'd always been afraid of mice. I imagined them racing toward me faster than my eyes could move, running up my body and around my collar bone, dragging their tails across my eyes. The fear ran deep, deep enough that I'd never been able to uproot it with the sharp but short spade of rational thinking.

One of the men dropped his pick axe and lunged toward the pair of runaways. He managed to capture the little one, which he carried away toward the woods.

"Don't separate the baby from its mother!" someone yelled.

Wanting to seem compassionate, and wanting to break away from Adrien's accusations, I decided to face my fears. I believed that I could. Following the other mouser's example, I went after the big one, scooping it up in my hands as if it were one of Adrien's kittens.

That's when it bit me. When I felt the

sting of the mother's teeth sink into the skin just below the base of my index fingernail, I flicked my right hand hard.

The mouse held on.

I flicked again, with all the force of my wrist and elbow, with enough force, I was sure, to slam this creature into the ground, breaking every delicate bone in its disgusting little body.

Still, the mouse held.

One more flick, and finally it sailed through the air and hit the ground running, not in the direction of the woods, but away from me, so I didn't care.

Suddenly I was the new cause for excitement. The boys gathered around to "ooh" and "ahh" at the liquid bubble of blood inflating near the tip of my finger. Then Adrien pushed through the crowd.

"Oh!" he cried, grabbing my wrist and pulling me in the direction of the first-aid tent. Someone caught up with us to pour a half bottle of water over my hand.

"It's not serious," I told them. But it was.

At the tent, Adrien explained the situation to the French doctor, gave me a peck on the forehead, and returned to the dig. I took that to mean our fight was over. My act of bravery had restored my virtue, at least for the moment. As the doctor treated my tiny wound with antibacterial ointment and a Band-Aid, did I know there was something that could not be so easily restored? Something like belief — in radical change, or radical love. Belief that Adrien, or anything, could transform me.

* * *

On Sunday, the first day of the summit, we awoke at 3 a.m., we ate, and we gathered. We chanted and blew whistles and marched in thousands toward Evian, hoping to block the paths of the conference attendees. We carried scrap wood to build a barricade, saline solution to clean our eyes, handkerchief masks to protect our lungs, cigarettes to calm our nerves. For all of these things we prepared, but at 3 a.m., at 4, at 5, the morning was still and bluish. The grasses lay still; the cows slept standing up.

Later, maybe at 7 or 8, when the blue light gave way to bright yellow, we encountered a blockade, rows of police in black uniforms and transparent masks, waving shields and firing canisters of tear gas high into the air.

Adrien called out over the noise of canisters clanking against the asphalt around our feet, "You want to advance?"

"Oui," I called back.

"Je t'aime," he said, pulling me close. We kissed through our handkerchiefs before running forward into the clouds, hurling rocks and used canisters in the direction of the police. Then we retreated, doused our eyes, and once again ran back for more, like children rushing in and out of icy sprinkler spray.

And all the while I felt a strange, irreverent separation from the mass. I knew there would be no revolution, no sudden about-face for me. I was caught instead on my own slow and halting march forward, a personal evolution that no one would celebrate with chanted rhymes or red flags. It was disappointing then. I had wanted to be swept away by something, to spiral out of control in the name of justice, or just romance. And many times I had — in the bedroom, in the stairwell. But every time, I had returned to me.

"Advance again?" Adrien shouted.

I secured my handkerchief and said, "Oui."

Contributors' Notes

Elizabeth M. Collins is an award-winning defense writer, sometime traveller, and new mother. She has a master's in nonfiction writing from Johns Hopkins and was the top civilian writer for the Department of Defense in 2012. Her work has appeared in newspapers and websites worldwide, and in *Outside In Literary and Travel Magazine*.

Vicki Valosik is a writer, sociologist, and synchronized swimmer based in Washington, D.C. Her work has appeared in publications such as *The Atlantic, Huffington Post, Washington Post Magazine, American Scholar, Philadelphia Inquirer, Washingtonian* and *International Educator*. Vicki also serves as Nonfiction Editor for *Outside In Literary & Travel Magazine*. More of her work can be found at vickivalosik.net.

Derek Perkins is an attorney by day and a moonlighting writer. He lives in South Carolina with his wife, daughter and their black Labrador retriever, Halo.

Bonnie Foote, PhD, taught English literature at UCLA before she switched to teaching yoga in Washington, D.C. She and her grandmother have travelled together through, in chronological order, Disneyland, Europe, Southeast Asia, Antarctica and West Africa.

Annie Mahon is a student, teacher and writer of mindfulness. She has been writing all her life, starting with her Dear Ziggy journal in junior high school, editing the University of Michigan Greek Newspaper, writing for the U-M yearbook and founding and editing the *Micro Digest*, the U-M Computing Center's first newsletter. More recently, she has become known for her monthly essays on mindfulness, a book of essays, *Thoughts from Annie*, and various articles on mindfulness and families. When not visiting her children, traveling the world, trying out new fitness modalities, writing or walking with her dogs, she practices yoga and mindfulness with her community at the Circle Yoga Cooperative in Washington, D.C.. Follow Annie's blog at http://rawmindfulness.com/.

Sylvia Bailey Shurbutt is Professor of English, Director of the Appalachian Heritage Writers Project and Coordinator of the Appalachian Studies Program at Shepherd University. She is managing editor of *The Anthology of Appalachian Writers* (ISSN 1946-3103). Her writing has appeared in *The Journal of Appalachian Studies, The Journal of Kentucky Studies, North Carolina Review, Women's Studies, Women and Language, Essays in Literature, The Southern Literary Journal* and *Scribner's American Writers and World Writers* series. Shurbutt was 2006 West Virginia Professor of the Year.

Marilyn Campbell is an award-winning feature writer whose work has appeared in *Connection Newspapers, The Florida Times Union, Outside In Literary & Travel Magazine* and the *Spinnaker.* She received an M.A. in writing from the Johns Hopkins University. She lives in Washington, D.C. with her husband and son.

Johanna Droubay lives with her husband and two children in northern Virginia. Her work has been published in *Willamette Week, Reed* magazine, and *Potomac Review*. She received a B.A. in English from Reed College and an M.A. in writing from Johns Hopkins. She works in communications at a high school.

About the Editor:

Meghan O'Neill is a style writer and non-fiction essayist. Her work has appeared in various magazines as well literary journals. Meghan lives in Maryland.

www.ingramcontent.com/pod-product-compliance
Lightning Source LLC
Chambersburg PA
CBHW031453040426
42444CB00007B/1081